Nepali Heritage

Celebrating Diversity in My Classroom

By Tamra B. Orr

21st Century Junior Library

Published in the United States of America by
Cherry Lake Publishing
Ann Arbor, Michigan
www.cherrylakepublishing.com

Reading Adviser: Cecilia Minden, PhD, Literacy expert and children's author

Photo Credits: ©Ocskay Bence/Shutterstock, cover; ©Arsgera/Shutterstock, 4; ©Serban Bogdan/Shutterstock, 6; ©Mila Supinskaya Glashchenko/Shutterstock, 8; ©dangdumrong/Shutterstock, 10; ©Alex Brylov/Shutterstock, 12; ©upslim/Shutterstock, 14; ©Pikoso.kz/Shutterstock, 16; ©Tomasz Wozniak/Shutterstock, 18; ©Zhuikova Alena/Shutterstock, 20

Library of Congress Cataloging-in-Publication Data
Name: Orr, Tamra, author.
Title: Nepali heritage / Tamra B. Orr.
Description: Ann Arbor : Cherry Lake, 2018. | Series: Celebrating diversity in my classroom | Includes bibliographical references and index.
Identifiers: LCCN 2018003272 | ISBN 9781534129047 (hardcover) | ISBN 9781534132245 (pbk.) | ISBN 9781534130746 (pdf) | ISBN 9781534133945 (hosted ebook)
Subjects: LCSH: Nepal–Juvenile literature.
Classification: LCC DS493.4 .O77 2018 | DDC 954.96–dc23
LC record available at https://lccn.loc.gov/2018003272

Cherry Lake Publishing would like to acknowledge the work of the Partnership for 21st Century Skills. Please visit *www.p21.org* for more information.

Printed in the United States of America
Corporate Graphics

CONTENTS

Nepal is home to Earth's highest peak, Mount Everest.

Noteworthy Nepal

Nepal is a small South Asian country that is 56,827 square miles (147,181 square kilometers) in size. It is just a little larger than Arkansas. But the country has 10 times the state's population.

In 2016, thousands of Nepalis **immigrated** to the United States. They experienced a terrible earthquake the year before. Many hope to return home once their country has had a chance to rebuild.

Nepal is located between China and India.
They are two of the world's largest countries.

Namaste!

Nepali is the official language of Nepal. It goes by many different names. It is also called Gurkha, Gorkahali, or Khaskura. Nepali is spoken in half of the country. **Dialects** change between western, eastern, and central Nepal. Also, royalty and members of the upper class use their own dialects. The other half of the population speak other languages. In fact, more than 123 languages are spoken throughout Nepal.

The word *Namaste* comes from Sanskrit. It is a very old language.

The word *Namaste* is used often in Nepal. It means both "hello" and "good-bye." People greet each other with this word. They usually place their palms together and bow their foreheads. The word translates to "I bow to you."

Think!

Nepalis have their own set of manners. For example, touching anything with your feet is **offensive**. The left hand can never be used for eating. You are not supposed to touch each other's head. That's because it is considered a **sacred** body part. Kissing in public is frowned upon. What are some of the manners you use on a daily basis? Do you know the reason behind each one?

Ganesha is the Hindu god of good fortune.

Doing the Right Thing

More than three-fourths of Nepalis are Hindu. The remaining are mostly Buddhist, Muslim, or Christian. In the Hindu religion, the one true God is Brahma. *Vedas* are ancient **scriptures** describing how people should live. The Hindu idea of *dharma* means to live a moral life. Hindus also believe souls are **immortal** and move from one body to another. This is known

Sherpas often don't make as much money as they deserve. They carry the heaviest things.

as **reincarnation**. How a person behaved in life is called *karma*. Karma affects how the soul comes back.

Most Nepalis live in the country's southern plains and central region. This includes the capital city of Kathmandu. The people who live in the mountains are *sherpas*. They are used to living in very high **elevations**. They are often hired to guide climbers up Nepal's soaring peaks.

Many Nepalese eat Dal Bhat with their fingers. They use their right hand.

Yogurt and Chutney

Nepal does not have an official national dish. If it did, most experts agree it would be *Dal Bhat*. The dish combines many of the country's favorite foods and flavors. Imagine a large platter with rice in the middle. It is surrounded by lentils, bowls of pickles, **curried** vegetables, and meat or fish. Finally, add two of the most common side dishes, yogurt and **chutney**. The entire meal

Momo are believed to be of Tibetan origin. Tibet is located above Nepal.

balances spicy and flavorful with mild and plain.

In Nepal, dumplings are called *momo*. They may contain meat, vegetables, or cheese. This snack is usually served on a plate with a few spicy dips. *Thukpa*, or noodle soup, is often eaten with the dumplings. Soup typically includes meat from a yak, goat, lamb, or chicken. Beef is never served because cows are considered sacred in Nepal. It is illegal to kill one.

Lake Phewa is the second largest lake in Nepal.

Water and Power

Life is quite simple in most parts of Nepal. It is one of the poorest countries in the world. Most of Nepal's electricity comes from **hydroelectric** power. This power is produced by the country's thousands of rivers and lakes. Often, there is not enough electricity for everyone. Many families go without any electricity for up to 8 hours a day, especially in winter. Also, most homes can only get

Guests in a Nepali household are not permitted to help cook or clean.

fresh water for 2 hours a day, 4 days a week. Polluted water has caused various diseases.

Despite these problems, the Nepalis are proud and welcome visitors. Sharing anything they have with others is one of their deeply held moral beliefs. A common phrase is, "Guests equals God."

Look!

Nepal is called "the Amazon of Asia" because its wildlife is so amazing. It has 870 **species** of birds and 650 species of butterflies. It also has 5,980 flowering plant species. What does this tell you about the country's climate and land?

INDEX

ABOUT THE AUTHOR

Tamra Orr is the author of hundreds of books for readers of all ages. She graduated from Ball State University, but moved with her husband and four children to Oregon in 2001. She is a full-time author, and when she isn't researching and writing books, she writes letters to friends all over the world. Orr enjoys life in the big city of Portland and feels very lucky to be surrounded by so much diversity.